Destination Hawaii

Written by Claire Owen

U.S.A.

My name is Alice. I live with my mom in San Francisco, and every year I visit my dad in Hawaii. Before I call Dad, I always figure out what time it is in Hawaii. Why don't all places around the world use the same time?

Contents

Wherever you see me, you'll find activities to try and questions to answer.

Aloha, Hawaii

Hawaii is the world's longest chain of islands, stretching for 1,523 miles in the Pacific Ocean. On a visit to Hawaii in 1866, author Mark Twain declared it to be "the loveliest fleet of islands that lies anchored in any ocean." Today, Hawaii is a popular vacation destination. Each year, millions of people are attracted by the islands' warm climate, beautiful scenery, friendly people, and some of the biggest waves in the world!

Did You Know?

Hawaii became the 50th state of the United States of America in 1959.

fleet   a group of ships sailing together

KAUAI

▲ Mt. Waialeale

NIIHAU

OAHU

PACIFIC OCEAN

○ Honolulu

MOLOKAI

MAUI

LANAI

KAHOOLAWE

Eight islands make up
nearly all of the land area
of Hawaii.

HAWAII
"The Big Island"

○ Hilo

Volcanoes
National Park

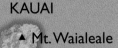

Visitors to Hawaii (2004)

Month	Visitors
January	516,953
February	536,167
March	583,915
April	548,599
May	549,865
June	616,023
July	683,006
August	645,543
September	526,602
October	560,134
November	526,661
December	622,433

Estimate and
then calculate the
total number of visitors
to Hawaii in 2004.
What was the average
number of visitors
per month?

5

Rising from the Sea

Hawaii is at the lower end of a chain of volcanoes that began to form more than 70 million years ago. Today, Hawaii still has five active volcanoes, although one of them will probably not reach sea level for another 250,000 years! At Volcanoes National Park, tourists can observe lava flows from Kilauea, the world's most active volcano.

Since Kilauea's latest series of eruptions began in 1983, lava flows have added more than 1,000 acres to the Big Island.

Molokini Crater is a dormant volcano about 12 miles from the island of Maui. The coral and sea life sheltered by the rim of the crater make this one of the world's best diving and snorkeling spots.

Koko Crater is a cone from the last volcano on Oahu to become extinct.

Mt. Everest is 29,035 feet high. Compare this with the height of Mauna Loa, when it is measured—
• from sea level.
• from the ocean floor.

Did You Know?

Mauna Loa, located on the Big Island, is the world's largest active volcano. It measures 18,000 feet from its base on the ocean floor to sea level, and another 13,677 feet to the summit.

7

Land of Contrasts

Most people associate Hawaii with warm, sunny weather.
It is true that many places in Hawaii have average maximum
temperatures in the 80s all year round. However, snow
falls most years on Hawaii's two highest volcanoes, and
the lowest temperature on record is a chilly 12°F. Hawaii's
rainfall is also variable. Mt. Waialeale (wy ah LAY ah LAY)
on the island of Kauai is the wettest place in the United
States, but other places in Hawaii receive only a few inches
of rain each year.

Hanauma Bay, Oahu

Mt. Waialeale (above);
Mauna Kea (left)

Waterfalls, Kauai (above);
Waimea Canyon (left)

Comparing Data

Although the average temperature and rainfall vary from place to place in Hawaii, there are some common patterns in the weather data. Temperatures are constant, rising by only a few degrees in the "summer" months from May to October. Rainfall is greatest in the "winter" months from November to April.

Honolulu

Jan	Feb	Mar	Apr	May	Jun	Jul	Aug	Sep	Oct	Nov	Dec
80	81	82	83	85	87	88	89	88	87	84	82
3.3	2.3	1.9	1.2	0.9	0.4	0.5	0.4	0.7	2.0	2.8	3.0

Ookala

Jan	Feb	Mar	Apr	May	Jun	Jul	Aug	Sep	Oct	Nov	Dec
77	77	77	77	79	80	81	81	82	81	79	77
9.9	10.7	13.9	15.2	8.9	4.7	8.2	9.6	5.1	7.4	12.2	11.9

Volcanoes National Park

Jan	Feb	Mar	Apr	May	Jun	Jul	Aug	Sep	Oct	Nov	Dec
67	67	67	67	69	70	71	72	72	72	69	67
13.3	10.2	12.5	10.7	7.3	4.9	6.3	7.0	5.4	6.8	13.3	11.6

KEY: ▢ Average Maximum Temperature (°F)   ▢ Average Rainfall (Inches)

Analyze Weather Data

To analyze the data on page 10, choose ONE of the tasks below. You will need a copy of the Blackline Master and a ruler.

1. Pick two or three of the places on page 10. Draw a line graph to show the temperatures for each place. (Use the temperature scale at the left.)

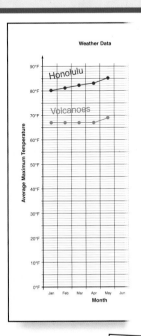

2. Pick two or three of the places on page 10. Draw a bar graph to show the rainfall for each place. (Use the rainfall scale at the right.)

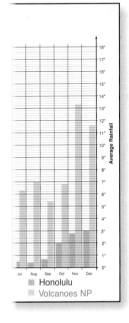

3. Pick one of the places on page 10. Draw a line graph to show the temperatures for that place. (Use the scale at the left.) On the same page, draw a bar graph to show the rainfall. (Use the scale at the right.)

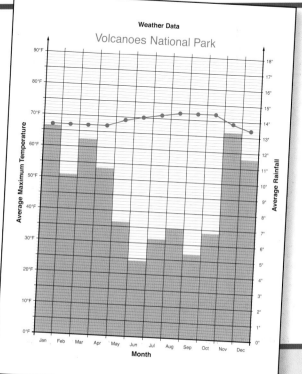

Travel Time

Hawaii is more than 2,000 miles from the nearest inhabited island and even farther from the other U.S. states. Flying from California to Honolulu takes about 5 hours. Traveling from the east coast usually involves several flights and can take up to 20 hours. By sea, the round trip from Los Angeles to Hawaii and back takes about 15 days.

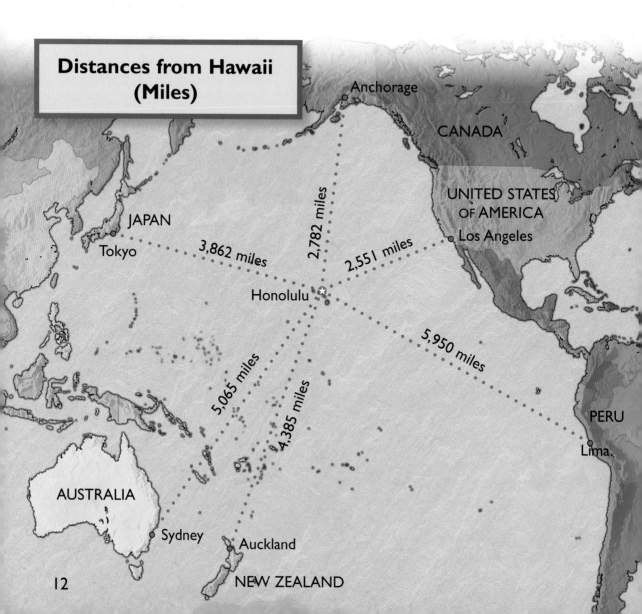

Distances from Hawaii (Miles)

Anchorage

CANADA

UNITED STATES OF AMERICA

Los Angeles

JAPAN

Tokyo

3,862 miles

2,782 miles

2,551 miles

Honolulu

5,950 miles

5,065 miles

4,385 miles

PERU

Lima

AUSTRALIA

Sydney

Auckland

NEW ZEALAND

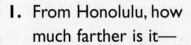

Figure It Out

In the 1920s, the only way to get to Hawaii was by sea. The Los Angeles Steamship Company charged between $325 and $635, per person, for the round trip.

1. From Honolulu, how much farther is it—

   a. to Anchorage compared to Los Angeles?

   b. to Lima than to Tokyo?

   c. to Sydney than to Auckland?

2. What is the total distance, via Honolulu—

   a. from Sydney to Los Angeles?

   b. from Tokyo to Lima?

   c. from Auckland to Anchorage?

3. Find the two distances on the map that have—

   a. the greatest difference.

   b. a total closest to 8,000 miles.

4. Estimate the average speed (in miles per hour) of—

   a. an airplane flying to Hawaii from Los Angeles.

   b. a ship cruising to Hawaii from Los Angeles.

ALOHA

Just arrived at the Hawaiian Islands Had a fine sea voyage

First Flights

The first nonstop flight to Hawaii was made by U.S. Army Air Corps pilot Lester Maitland and navigator Albert Hegenberger. Their aircraft, named *Bird of Paradise*, departed from Oakland, California, on June 28, 1927. It landed 25 hours and 50 minutes later on the island of Oahu.

On January 10 and 11, 1935, Amelia Earhart made the first solo flight across the Pacific by a woman. She flew from Hawaii to California.

The *Bird of Paradise* landed on Oahu at 6:29 A.M. on June 29. At what time on June 28 did the airplane take off from Oakland?

The China Clipper was the first commercial aircraft to fly to Hawaii. The inventor of the China Clipper, Glenn Martin (right), is shown with a model of the transpacific aircraft on his desk.

HAWAII
BY CLIPPER

PAN AMERICAN WORLD AIRWAYS
The System of the Flying Clippers

PAN-AMERICAN AIRWAYS "CHINA CLIPPER" ARRIVES AT SAN FRANCISCO, FROM THE ORIENT

© CLYDE SUNDERLAND

In October 1936, nine airline passengers traveled to Honolulu on the luxurious China Clipper. They each paid $1,438.20 for the round trip from San Francisco to the Philippines. This was a huge amount of money in the days when many Americans earned less than $20 per week.

Hawaiian Time

Many visitors to Hawaii need a few days to adjust to the different time zone. Someone from Los Angeles might not be affected much by the two-hour time difference. However, a visitor from New York, where the time is five hours ahead of Hawaiian time, would probably find it difficult to stay awake at eight o'clock on a Honolulu evening!

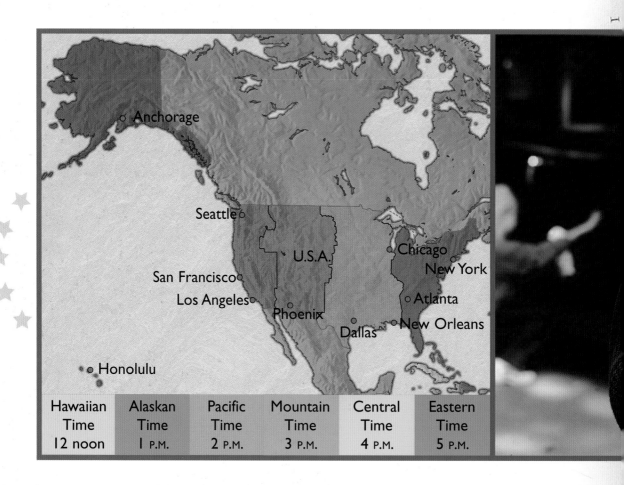

Hawaiian Time	Alaskan Time	Pacific Time	Mountain Time	Central Time	Eastern Time
12 noon	1 P.M.	2 P.M.	3 P.M.	4 P.M.	5 P.M.

time zone   any of the 24 longitudinal divisions of Earth's surface
that has its own time

Hawaii

The pictures below show a four-way telephone call. In which time zones are the people in pictures A, B, and C?

A

B

Pick two places (D and E) in different time zones. What time is it in Place D when the time in Place E is—
- 6 P.M.?
- 4 A.M.?
- 12 noon?

C

Standard Time

In the days before standard time, cities would set their town clocks according to the position of the sun. The time in one city could be a few minutes different from the time in another city only 30 or 40 miles away. This did not matter in the days before it was possible to travel quickly from place to place. However, when the cities became linked by railroads, these time differences began to cause problems.

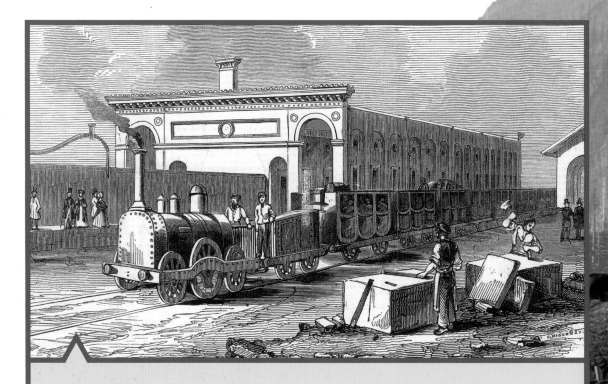

In the 1840s, England's railroad stations adopted London time. To use the railroads, people needed to know exactly what time the trains would arrive and depart. For this reason, towns and cities all over England began setting their clocks to London time.

standard time   the official time for any of the 24 time zones

It would be impractical for the huge continent of North America to have only one time zone. On November 18, 1883, U.S. and Canadian railroad companies adopted standard one-hour time zones similar to those used today.

World Time Zones

In 1884, delegates from 27 nations met in Washington and extended the North American system of time zones to the rest of the world. First, the world was divided into 24 one-hour time zones of equal width. Then the shape of the zones was adjusted so that they followed the borders of countries or states. All time zones were measured from the prime meridian, an imaginary line that passes through Greenwich, near London, England.

Visitors to Greenwich like to stand with one foot on either side of the prime meridian!

delegate   a person who is sent to represent the views of a group

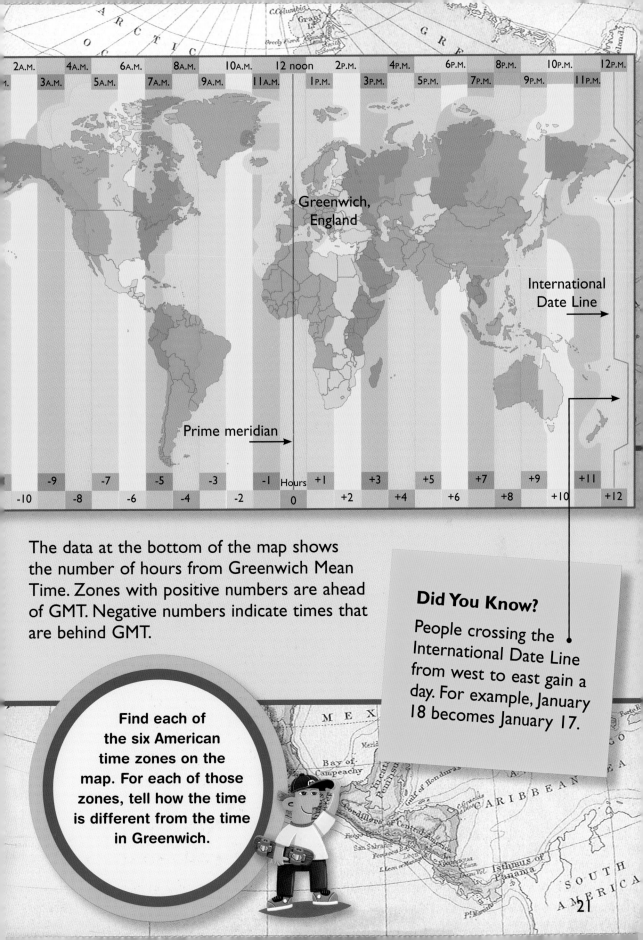

| 2A.M. | 4A.M. | 6A.M. | 8A.M. | 10A.M. | 12 noon | 2P.M. | 4P.M. | 6P.M. | 8P.M. | 10P.M. | 12P.M. |

| 3A.M. | 5A.M. | 7A.M. | 9A.M. | 11A.M. | 1P.M. | 3P.M. | 5P.M. | 7P.M. | 9P.M. | 11P.M. |

Greenwich, England

International Date Line

Prime meridian

| -9 | | -7 | | -5 | | -3 | | -1 | Hours | +1 | | +3 | | +5 | | +7 | | +9 | | +11 | |
| -10 | -8 | | -6 | | -4 | | -2 | | 0 | | +2 | | +4 | | +6 | | +8 | | +10 | | +12 |

The data at the bottom of the map shows the number of hours from Greenwich Mean Time. Zones with positive numbers are ahead of GMT. Negative numbers indicate times that are behind GMT.

Did You Know?

People crossing the International Date Line from west to east gain a day. For example, January 18 becomes January 17.

Find each of the six American time zones on the map. For each of those zones, tell how the time is different from the time in Greenwich.

21

Flying Time

Working with times in two different time zones requires a little care. Alice is flying from California to Hawaii. Her ticket shows that she leaves San Francisco at 4:15 P.M. and arrives in Honolulu at 7:35 P.M. She wants to figure out how long the flight will take.

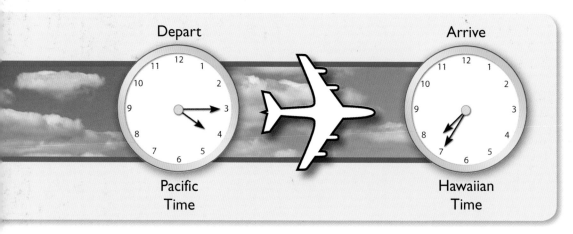

Depart — Pacific Time

Arrive — Hawaiian Time

Alice knows that Hawaiian Time is 2 hours behind Pacific Time. When her 4:15 flight leaves San Francisco, the time in Honolulu will be 2:15 P.M.

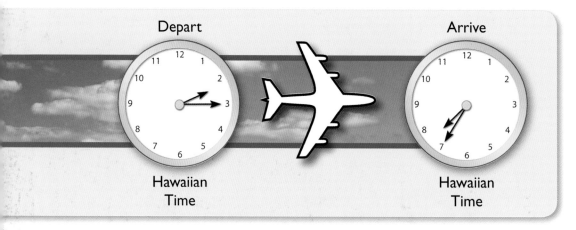

Depart — Hawaiian Time

Arrive — Hawaiian Time

Alice can now see that her flight will take 5 hours and 20 minutes.

Figure out the flying time for each of these nonstop flights. (Use the time-zone map on page 16 to help.)

E Depart Honolulu: 10:59 P.M.
   Arrive Anchorage: 6:44 A.M.

Honolulu

B Depart Chicago: 9:15 A.M.
   Arrive Honolulu: 1:45 P.M.

A Depart Los Angeles: 8:10 A.M.
   Arrive Honolulu: 11:40 A.M.

D Depart Honolulu: 2:22 P.M.
   Arrive Phoenix: 11:27 P.M.

C Depart Atlanta: 10:50 A.M.
   Arrive Honolulu: 3:15 P.M.

Sample Answers

> Make up some other problems that involve traveling to Hawaii. For example, you could tell the departure time and flight length and ask a partner to figure out the arrival time.

Page 5 6,915,901; about 576,325

Page 7 Everest is 15,358 feet higher.
Mauna Loa is 2,642 feet higher.

Page 13 1. a. 231 miles   b. 2,088 miles
c. 680 miles

2. a. 7,616 miles   b. 9,812 miles
c. 7,167 miles

3. a. 5,950 – 2,551 = 3,399 miles
b. 5,065 + 2782 = 7,847 miles

4. a. about 510 mph
b. about 14 mph

Page 14 4:39 A.M.

Page 17 A. Mountain Time   B. Alaskan Time
C. Eastern Time

Page 21 Zones range from 10 hours behind Greenwich
(Hawaiian Time) to 5 hours behind (Eastern Time).

Page 23 A. 5 hours, 30 minutes   B. 8 hours, 30 minutes
C. 9 hours, 25 minutes   D. 6 hours, 5 minutes
E. 6 hours, 45 minutes

Index